nden

FROM FARM TO FORK

Where Do Grains Come From?

Linda Staniford

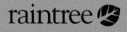

raintree

a Capstone company — publishers for children

Raintree is an imprint of Capstone Global Library Limited, a company incorporated in England and Wales having its registered office at 264 Banbury Road, Oxford, OX2 7DY – Registered company number: 6695582

www.raintree.co.uk
myorders@raintree.co.uk

Edited by Helen Cox Cannons
Designed by Steve Mead
Original illustrations © Capstone Global Library Limited 2016
Illustrated by Steve Mead
Picture research by Tracy Cummins
Production by Victoria Fitzgerald
Originated by Capstone Global Library Limited
Printed and bound in China

ISBN 978 1 4747 2120 2
20 19 18 17 16
10 9 8 7 6 5 4 3 2 1

British Library Cataloguing in Publication Data
A full catalogue record for this book is available from the British Library.

Acknowledgements
We would like to thank the following for permission to reproduce photographs: Alamy: Design Pics Inc, 9, imageBROKER, 15; Getty Images: Bill Hogan/Chicago Tribune/MCT, 20, BRIGITTE WEIDLICH/AFP, 7; Shutterstock: Alvin Terry, 12, Andrii Bielov, 5, Artens, 19, ArtThailand, 11, BLUR LIFE 1975, 16, D.Shashikant, 22 Top, Daniele Silva, 13, Diana Taliun, 23 Bottom, Elena Schweitzer, 23 Middle, Focon, 18, Iasmina Calinciuc, 17, Jimmy Tran, Cover Back, 10, MOSO IMAGE, Cover Right, PunyaFamily, 8, puwanai, 14, Spaceport9, Cover Left, Sunny Forest, 4, Tish1, 6, vry, 21.

Every effort has been made to contact copyright holders of material reproduced in this book. Any omissions will be rectified in subsequent printings if notice is given to the publisher.

All the internet addresses (URLs) given in this book were valid at the time of going to press. However, due to the dynamic nature of the internet, some addresses may have changed, or sites may have changed or ceased to exist since publication. While the author and publisher regret any inconvenience this may cause readers, no responsibility for any such changes can be accepted by either the author or the publisher.

Some words are shown in bold, **like this**. You can find out what they mean by looking in the glossary.

Contents

What are grains?

Grains are small, hard, dry seeds. They come from grass-like plants such as wheat and barley. Grains are the part of a plant that can grow to make a new plant.

Grains are the main part of people's diets all over the world. Grains are also called **cereals**.

Where do grains grow?

corn

Grains are grown all over the world.
Wheat, oats, barley and corn (maize) all
grow in the United States and Europe.

millet

Millet is a type of grain that grows in Africa. Rice grows in tropical countries such as China and India. In this book we will look at how rice gets from farms to your plate.

How is rice planted?

In Asia, rice seeds are planted in a seedbed. The seeds grow into rice plants. When they are big enough, the seeds are planted in **flooded** fields called paddy fields.

In other countries, rice seeds are
sometimes loaded into aeroplanes.
The aeroplanes fly over the paddy fields
and drop the seeds from the air.

How does rice grow?

The paddy fields are kept full of water. As the rice plants get bigger, the water level goes down.

The rice plants grow quickly. They make seed heads that contain grains of rice.

How is rice harvested?

When the rice grains are ripe, the paddy field is drained so that it is dry. In Asia, the rice is often harvested by hand. Workers cut the stalks and put them into **bundles**.

Harvesting is done by machines on large rice farms. The machines cut and bundle the rice.

What happens to the rice after harvesting?

The rice is then beaten. This separates the rice grain from the rest of the plant. This is called **threshing**. Threshing can be done by hand or by machine.

The rice grains are then dried in the sun or in large driers. This stops the rice from rotting.

How is rice processed?

Rice grains have a hard, outer shell that we cannot eat. The grains are **milled**, or ground, to remove this shell.

After milling, the grains are brown.
They have a layer of bran on the outside.
Some rice is milled again to become
white rice.

What happens to the rice next?

The rice is put into bags and loaded onto lorries. It is then taken to shops and markets.

Some rice is also taken to ports. At the
ports, the rice is loaded into **cargo ships**.
The ships take the rice to countries where
rice does not grow.

How does rice reach us?

Workers put the bags of rice onto shelves in shops. There are different kinds of rice. Long grain, short grain and basmati are kinds of rice.

Rice is often eaten in side dishes, in paellas, in Asian dishes or in curries. The rice has had a long journey from farm to fork!

All kinds of grains!

Maize, wheat and rice are the most commonly grown grain crops in the world. Wheat gives us flour to make bread, pasta and noodles.

Quinoa and barley are healthy grains. They are good for you.

Brown rice is a **whole-grain** food. Whole-grain foods include the bran and wheatgerm. Whole-grain foods are good for you.

Glossary

bundle number of things tied or wrapped up together

cargo ship very large ship that carries goods from one country to another

cereals edible grains that come from grass-like plants such as wheat, oats and rice

flood cover over with water

milled ground in a mill

threshing beating or rubbing the grain to separate seeds from a harvested plant

whole-grain foods that are whole-grain have the bran and wheatgerm from a grain in them

Find out more

Books

All About Cereals (Food Zone), Victoria Parker (QEB
  Publishing, 2010)
Food from Farms (World of Farming), Nancy Dickmann
  (Raintree, 2010)

Websites

**https://learnenglishkids.britishcouncil.org/en/
category/topics/food**
This website contains lots of fun, food-based games for
you to play.

Index